Jellyfish John
&
The Eight Thinking Caps

By Deana Bamford
Art by Nicola Tebbutt

Copyright © 2024 by Deana Bamford.

All rights reserved. This book or any portion thereof may not be reproduced or used in any manner whatsoever without the express written permission of the publisher, except for the use of brief quotations in a book review.

Published in the United Kingdom by
Coalville C.A.N. Community Publishing
Memorial Square,
Coalville,
Leicestershire,
England,
LE67 3TU

First Published in 2020
ISBN 978-1-9168960-1-7

Second Edition
10 9 8 7 6 5 4 3 2 1

https://coalvilleccp.uk

This is the tale of
Jellyfish John
and
he hopes it's useful to you!

By sharing his story and
having some fun he wants to help in all
that you do.

You see for Jellyfish John life wasn't always so great, he used to feel worthless and scared.

When things were confused in his head, he'd get mad and glow red, he felt as if nobody cared.

He'd scream and shout, and without caring about the people around him he'd sting.

Fed up of being chastised, he soon realised, that he needed some different thinking!

One night in a dream...
He witnessed a scene from a story
that grabbed his attention.
It told of 8 caps, that came in a rap,
to avoid mistakes and detention.

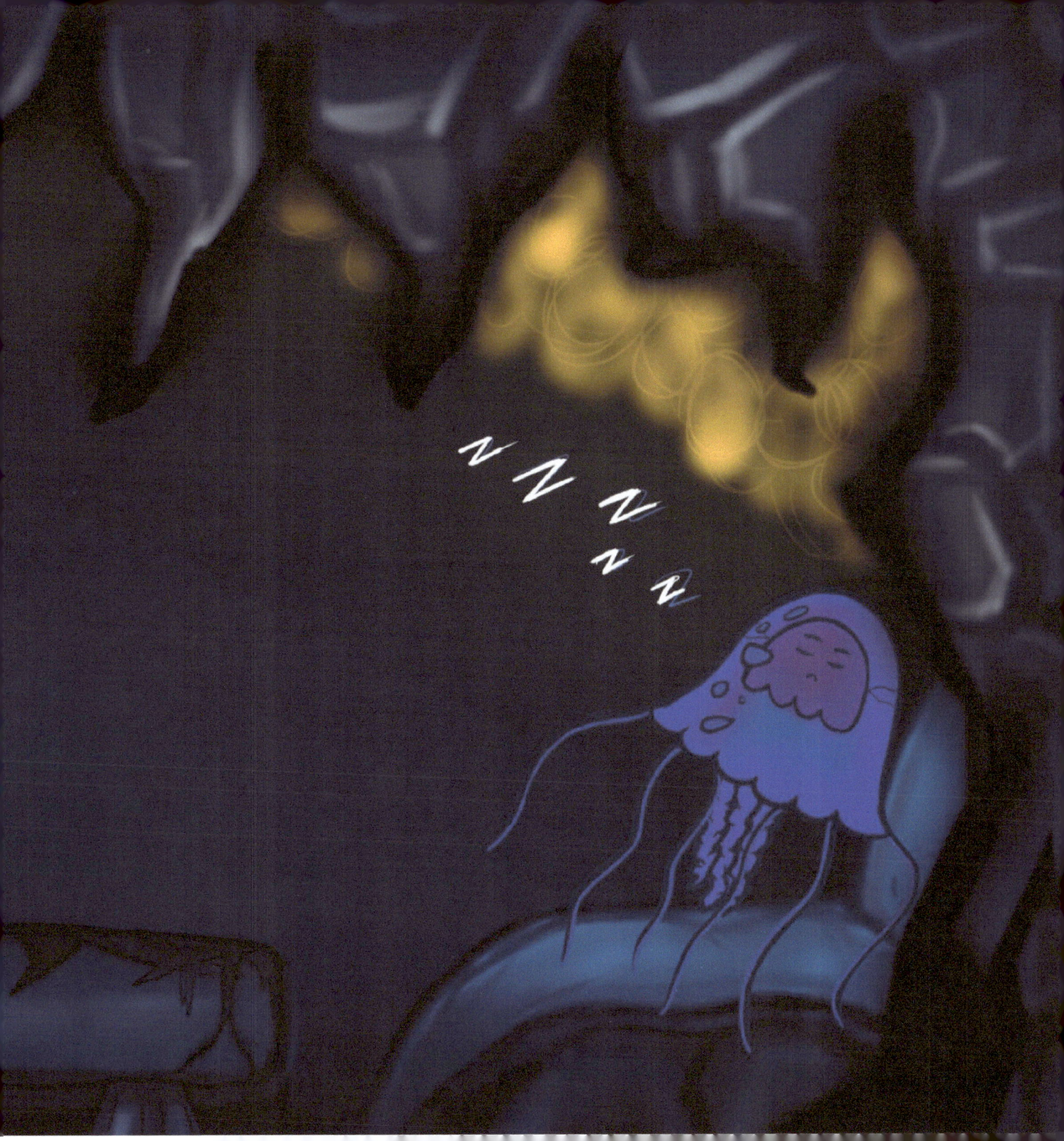

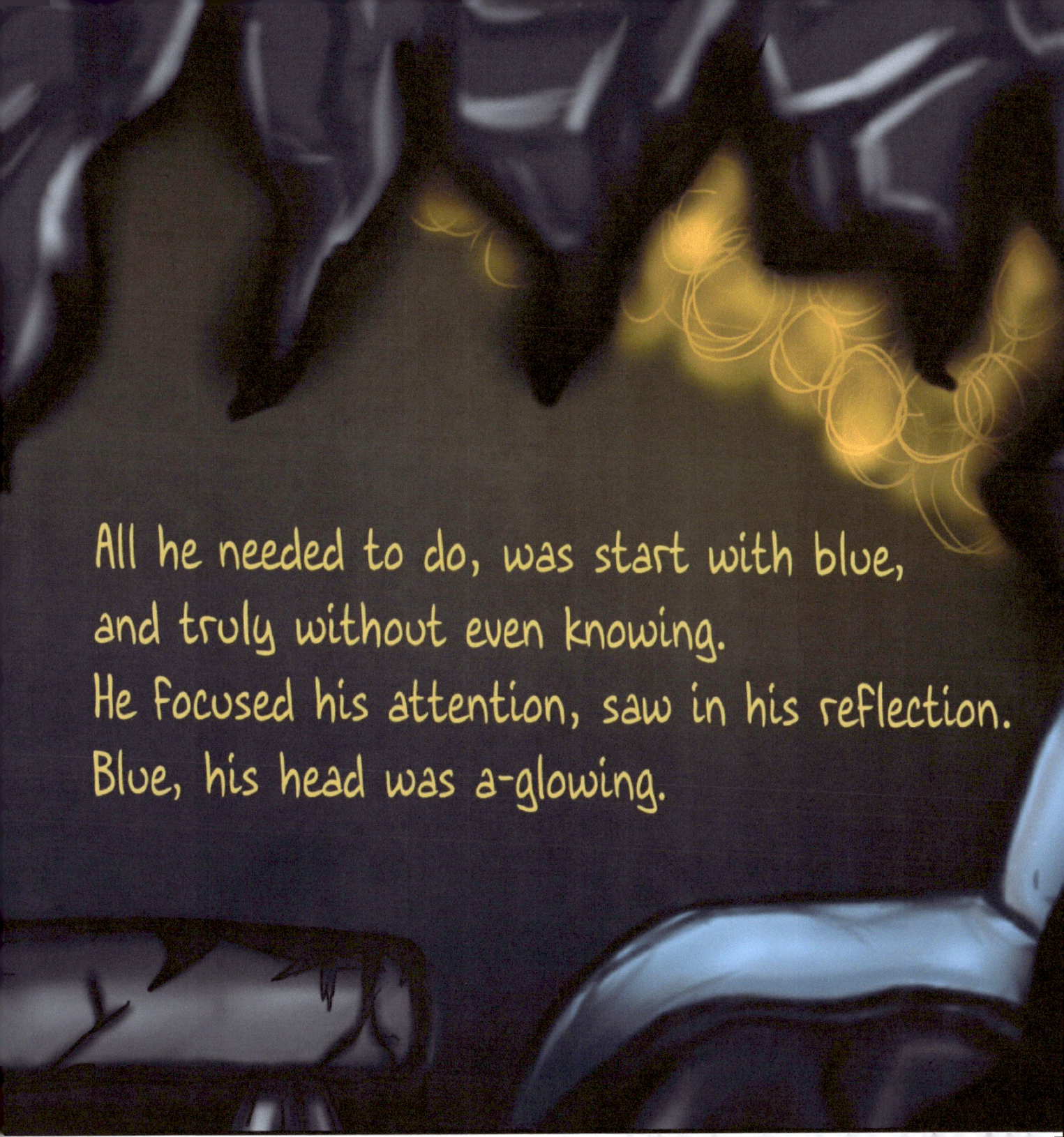

All he needed to do, was start with blue,
and truly without even knowing.
He focused his attention, saw in his reflection.
Blue, his head was a-glowing.

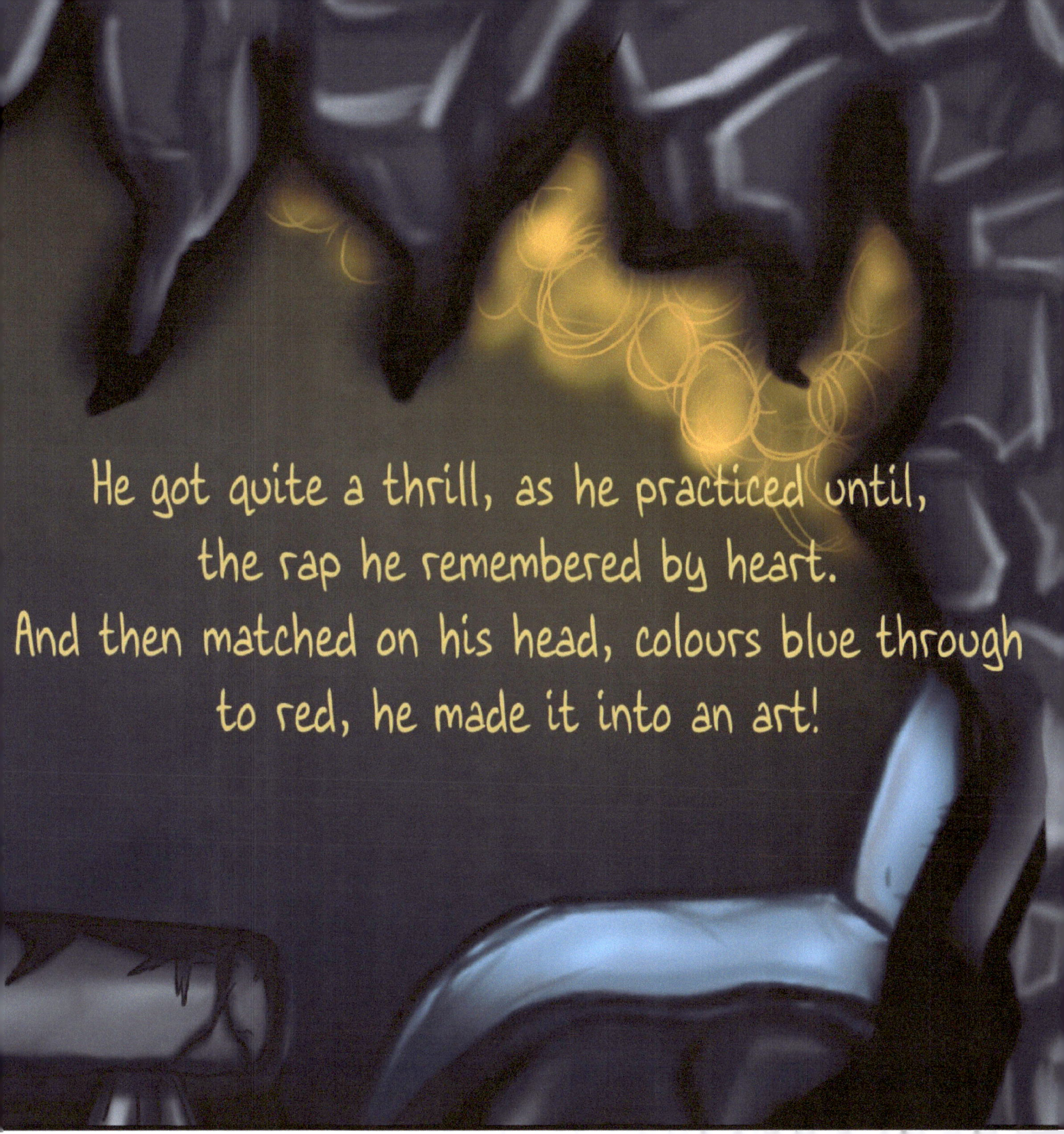

He got quite a thrill, as he practiced until,
the rap he remembered by heart.
And then matched on his head, colours blue through
to red, he made it into an art!

He realised this skill, was special to him, he decided to make some amends.

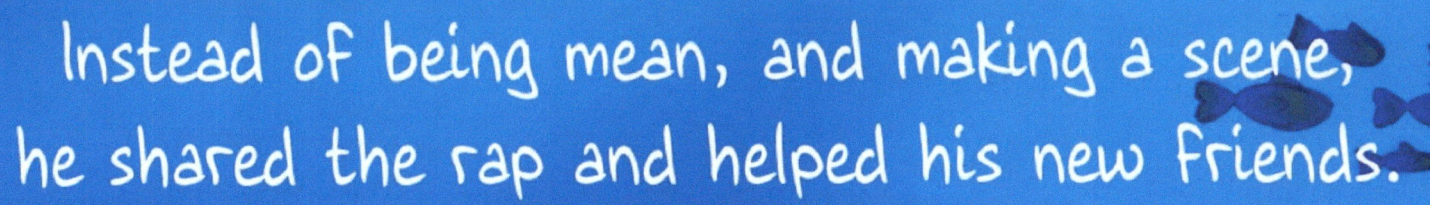
Instead of being mean, and making a scene, he shared the rap and helped his new friends.

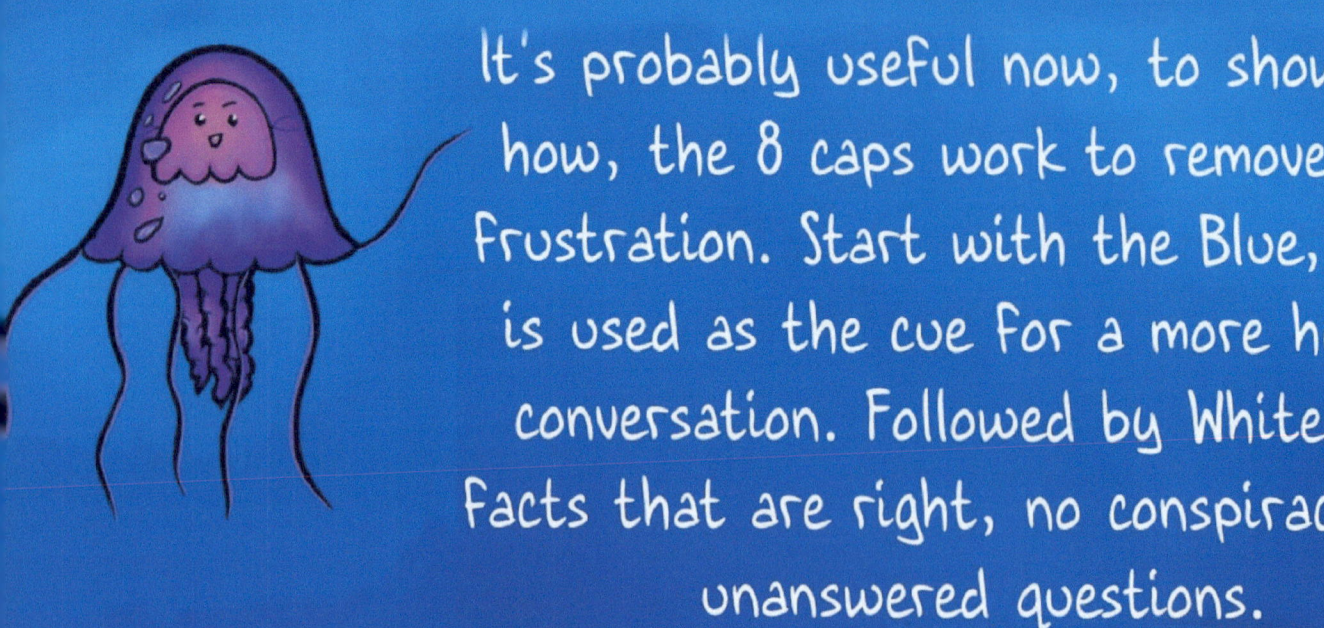

It's probably useful now, to show you how, the 8 caps work to remove your frustration. Start with the Blue, which is used as the cue for a more helpful conversation. Followed by White, the facts that are right, no conspiracies or unanswered questions.

The final two, Purple and Gold just for you, wear them to decide what action to take. Listen to others perspectives, just be more effective, a better future you'll help to create.

So John took control, embraced his new role,
he became the problem solver 'go-to'.
When there was anger and doubt, or arguments
broke out, everyone knew what they needed to
do.

Olly and her crew, were arguing too, about bedtime, homework and reading.

When the 8 caps were done, they all felt like they'd won, they sorted it out between them.

Salty and Curly kept falling out, about their boat and a recent crash landing.

When Nancy and her mates, concerned at the state, of the rubbish dumped in the ocean...

John shared what to do, they all talked it through, and a plan they put into motion.

"You can use them yourself
you can share them with others
If you don't need them all
Just select the right colours"

"With special thanks to our friend Jellyfish John with the 8 cap rap.
Our troubles are gone"
So that's the story of Jellyfish John, use it and share it - His 8 cap song

The 8 Cap Rap

The first ones blue, this is for you
Make a TH!NKing plan, don't forget for who
You're in charge, show some respect
Blue caps the boss, right left, right left

Next ones white, facts to delight
Just evidence ok, no guessing right?
If no-one knows or you disagree
Then you'll know exactly what facts you need

Then comes the red, get your feelings out
Don't be led, its a release no doubt
Can't keep it in? get some magic potion
Red cap on – share your emotion

Blacks next in line, take care, don't fret
An essential cap to place on your head
Keep it on to get the issues down
Don't let it stick, you don't want to drown

Come on the yellow, this cap you'll see
Contains good stuff and positivity
Benefits, bonuses, things that are great
Get 'em all out, don't hesitate

Ideas abound, no wrong answers,
With the green cap on, be the ideas master
Keep on going, you can't think of enough
Enjoy the feeling, the buzz, the right stuff

So gold is the one, what action to take
Just the first step you might make
To keep it going, and start your journey
You're in control, you have power of attorney

Purples the last cap you wear
With the others, think to whom you'll share
Fulfil your dreams, avoid a nightmare
With your 8 cap rap, don't get stuck, take care

- CATCHY CHORUS! -

With your 8 caps to hand, there are no limits
Once inside, no need for gimmicks
Gotta recognise your power, your credentials
Connect with others, unleash your potential

So keep them to hand and share them wide
Together there'll be no place to hide - For negative ninnies - need more convincing?
Time to join the revolution in TH!NKing

The Eight Thinking Caps

Co-ordinate

Blue Cap
Decides what thinking is needed and when.

Good Stuff

Yellow Cap
All the postives.

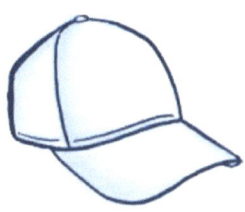

Evidence

White Cap
Focus on the facts and truth.

Possibilities

Green Cap
Possibilities, Ideas, new/fresh thinking and solutions.

Emotions

Red Cap
To describe feelings about the situation.

Connect

Purple Cap
Who with and when will I share?

Caution

Black Cap
What are the downsides?

Action

Gold Cap
What will I do now?

Now it's your turn!
Think of a problem you've had recently, write it down and think of which caps would be helpful to you and your situation.

___

___

___

___

___

___

___

___

___

___

___

www.ingramcontent.com/pod-product-compliance
Lightning Source LLC
Chambersburg PA
CBHW041539040426
42446CB00002B/156